Hell, I Love Everybody

Also by James Tate

Hell, I Love Everybody

The Essential James Tate

Poems

James Tate

Edited by Dara Barrois/Dixon,
Emily Pettit, and Kate Lindroos

An Imprint of HarperCollins*Publishers*

HarperCollins books may be purchased for educational, business, or sales promotional use. For information, please email the Special Markets Department at SPsales@harpercollins.com.

Ecco® and HarperCollins® are trademarks of HarperCollins Publishers.

FIRST EDITION

Designed by Jennifer Chung

Library of Congress Cataloging-in-Publication Data has been applied for.

ISBN 978-0-06-330607-3

23 24 25 26 27 LBC 5 4 3 2 1

Contents

Foreword

The ideal annual reading of James Tate's *Hell, I Love Everybody* begins with die-hard fans volunteering wide-ranging accounts of their James Tate encounters. Readers recall where they were and what they felt hearing lines of the fifty-two poems in *Hell, I Love Everybody*. Most refer to the late poet as "Jim." Only familiarity with the defamiliarizing feel of a Tate poem prepares a newcomer for one of these annual readings. Someone once read "I Left My Couch in Tatamagouche" over the beat of A Tribe Called Quest's "I Left My Wallet in El Segundo" at an event. Someone else claims to have heard Bill Murray read "The Blue Booby" under Brooklyn Bridge in the rainy season.

When the book event occurs in an abandoned zoo or bus depot, a policeman with a goat named "the Prince of Peace" usually makes a cameo. Some readers insist Tate appears disguised as the policeman or goat. When the book event happens near a river, some readers come dressed as toads. Marguerite Farnish Burridge and her husband, Knelm Oswald Lancelot Burridge, claimed to have attended a library reading where when Tate said, "A book can move from room to room without anyone touching it," all the spines on the shelves and chairs shuddered. (The two agree they also saw Muhammad Ali levitate in a Four Seasons hotel hallway.) I tell the reader next to me that I found Tate all by myself in a Hartsville, South Carolina, bookstore in 1991. "I Am a Finn," the reader replies, knowing.

Four muscular readers grab the corners of the portable stage, carrying it from the riverbank to the barn while the elderly woman on the stage recalls hearing Tate read "Where Babies Come From" at her sister's baby shower. Who was the baby? "David Berman," I shout from the crowd. The woman looks to see who said this and makes an unreadable face. "When Jim said our parents almost always stood on the wrong shore, we heard waves crashing though we were indoors," she says, nearly toppling from the stagehands. Stan, a grizzled community college creative writing professor, claims to have organized a minor junior faculty rebellion after Tate read "How the Pope Is Chosen." At some events two readers stage a reading of "The Rules," standing at opposite sides of the event space shouting lines through bullhorns while readers in the audience repeat them.

The subtextual pang you find in a Jim Tate line, a deadpan panic, creeps into the echoes.

Tate seemed always to be saying someone else is saying something in his poems. He was a ventriloquist and witness. Somewhere there is voice-over bootleg footage of Jim Tate saying, "I'm just a hungry little Gnostic in need of a sandwich." The Tate poem makes the dark and unknown as illuminating as the enlightened and logical. In a poem, "Just as many things exist in the dark as they do in the light."

When Tate said to a team of junior gymnasts snowed in at a diner, "My felisberto is handsomer than your mergotroid," there was, according to Jemma, one of the gymnasts, an outbreak of laughter so contagious, Mr. Tate could not finish his poem. Jemma who was so moved by Tate's unfinished reading, she began the Jim Tate Reading Club for Gymnasts and Fans. Fans, coaches, opponents and their coaches and fans, and anyone in attendance with interest may join Jemma's Jim Tate Reading Club for Gymnasts and Fans, now in year three and going strong.

The Tate poem is full of comedic timing and obsessive timekeeping. The Charlie Chaplin–like poet displaced to contemporary middle American ennui and deluded, denuded delight. Like the deadpan voice-over of a Charlie Kaufman high school hooky movie. Tate appears disguised as Charlie Brown or Charlie Parker. Tate appears disguised as a candy store shopkeeper impervious to ill will, a blue antelope, a woodpecker tapping Morse code into a dead oak tree, a pink-eyed extraterrestrial infatuated with John Ford Westerns. Tate's poems induce imaginative fortitude. Events can happen in a mind, a mine, or a minefield, ideally when the temperate outdoors and indoors are the same.

When a reader contemplates leaving the book party, the reader who notices must say, "I feel as if I were the residue of a stranger's life, that I should pursue you." The Jim Tate poem normalizes the bizarre, the dream-songy, the mythic, the absurd, the quotidian, the diurnal, surreal, and occasionally nightmarish feeling of life. "This is a house of unwritten poems, this is where I am unborn," Tate tells readers in a room below a falling darkness, and then for years and years someone reads him saying it at a book party or alone at home. It's truly wonderful to read in a James Tate voice alone or at public, private, or secret reading. Adjust your tongue so that it can hold a small key underneath. Adjust the ear at the back of your neck and the eye at the tip of your nose. Speak like a lost pilot in a lost key. Everyone is expected to read.

—*Terrance Hayes*

Editor's Note

We began with the usual apprehension over eliminating poems and pages. "We" being Kate Lindroos, poet, essayist, and historian; and Emily Pettit, poet, artist, and James Tate's stepdaughter; and me. We wanted to assemble a book that serves the elemental purpose of a love for keeping poetry nearby. We looked for a book matching as much as possible the big openheartedness throughout James Tate's life-long dedication to poetry.

We understood the word *essential*, while inviting assurances of decisiveness and comprehensive selection, did not require us to focus on exclusion over inclusion. Once we realized this, the pleasure of thinking of what to include resembled the pleasure poetry provides when it helps us feel how open our minds can be, how pleasing thinking along with another's mind can be, and how poetry lends us opportunities to think through what otherwise might not have occurred to us to explore.

A poem in Tate's first book says . . . *I would have lent you sugar* . . . and this is what we hope to do, as well, in spirit. We invoke the generosity of Tate's poems.

We took three years to read Tate's books, consider selections, talk about purposes, arrive at potential tables of contents, propose new selections, come at selections from different angles, try out new tables of contents, and settle on the book you may be about to read. Sometimes we agonized. Many times we remembered how magical it felt to read one of the poems for the first time. We went from around 180 poems selected, to 90, to 52. It sometimes felt like a betrayal to leave out a poem so many of us have loved. But we wanted to make an intimate book. A comprehensive or complete collection of Tate's poems, when one comes, will be another kind of book, valuable in other ways.

We've put together a book of beloved favorites. We imagine someone saying as they give or lend the book to a friend, a stranger, a beloved, an acquaintance: *Here, take this book, read these poems, you'll love this poet.*

We thank the openheartedness of other readers who contributed to our considerations, namely Rachel B. Glaser, Lesle Lewis, Guy Pettit, James Haug, Jamie Thomson, Brian Henry, John Emil Vincent. A special section at jamestate.net includes the names of others who chose Tate poems to highlight and for our consideration. We thank all these and others and all our friends and family who let us know some of their favorite poems. We also thank Gabriella Doob of Ecco and Cora Markowitz of the Georges Borchardt Agency for their guidance and enthusiasm. To everyone who reaches for poetry for their own reasons, this book is dedicated to you.

—Dara Barrois/Dixon

Acknowledgments

Academy of American Poets; *American Poetry Review*; *Atlantic Monthly Press*; *Believer Magazine*; *Conduit*; *Conjunctions*; Ecco/HarperCollins; *Great American Prose Poems*; Harry Ransom Center; *The Iowa Review*; jamestate.net; *jubilat*; Little, Brown and Company; The University of Massachusetts Press; *The New Yorker*; *The North American Review*; *The Paris Review*; *PN Review*; *Poetry*; *Poetry Now*; Sarabande Books; Scram Press; Shepherd's Press; *Verse*; Wesleyan University Press; Yale University Press.

Hell, I Love Everybody

Goodtime Jesus

Jesus got up one day a little later than usual. He had been dreaming so deep there was nothing left in his head. What was it? A nightmare, dead bodies walking all around him, eyes rolled back, skin falling off. But he wasn't afraid of that. It was a beautiful day. How 'bout some coffee? Don't mind if I do. Take a little ride on my donkey, I love that donkey. Hell, I love everybody.

The Blue Booby

The blue booby lives
on the bare rocks
of Galápagos
and fears nothing.
It is a simple life:
they live on fish,
and there are few predators.
Also, the males do not
make fools of themselves
chasing after the young
ladies. Rather,
they gather the blue
objects of the world
and construct from them

a nest—an occasional
Gauloises package,
a string of beads,
a piece of cloth from
a sailor's suit. This

replaces the need for
dazzling plumage;
in fact, in the past
fifty million years
the male has grown
considerably duller,
nor can he sing well.
The female, though,

asks little of him—
the blue satisfies her
completely, has
a magical effect
on her. When she returns
from her day of
gossip and shopping,
she sees he has found her
a new shred of blue foil:
for this she rewards him
with her dark body,
the stars turn slowly
in the blue foil beside them
like the eyes of a mild savior.

The Promotion

I was a dog in my former life, a very good
dog, and, thus, I was promoted to a human being.
I liked being a dog. I worked for a poor farmer
guarding and herding his sheep. Wolves and coyotes
tried to get past me almost every night, and not
once did I lose a sheep. The farmer rewarded me
with good food, food from his table. He may have
been poor, but he ate well. And his children
played with me, when they weren't in school or
working in the field. I had all the love any dog
could hope for. When I got old, they got a new
dog, and I trained him in the tricks of the trade.
He quickly learned, and the farmer brought me into
the house to live with them. I brought the farmer
his slippers in the morning, as he was getting
old, too. I was dying slowly, a little bit at a
time. The farmer knew this and would bring the
new dog in to visit me from time to time. The
new dog would entertain me with his flips and
flops and nuzzles. And then one morning I just

didn't get up. They gave me a fine burial down
by the stream under a shade tree. That was the
end of my being a dog. Sometimes I miss it so
I sit by the window and cry. I live in a high-rise
that looks out at a bunch of other high-rises.
At my job I work in a cubicle and barely speak
to anyone all day. This is my reward for being
a good dog. The human wolves don't even see me.
They fear me not.

Consumed

Why should you believe in magic,
pretend an interest in astrology
or the tarot? Truth is, you are

free, and what might happen to you
today, nobody knows. And your
personality may undergo a radical

transformation in the next half
hour. So it goes. You are consumed
by your faith in justice, your

hope for a better day, the rightness
of fate, the dreams, the lies
the taunts.—Nobody gets what he

wants. A dark star passes through
you on your way home from
the grocery: never again are you

the same—an experience which is
impossible to forget, impossible
to share. The longing to be pure

is over. You are the stranger
who gets stranger by the hour.

Rapture

"If you sit here a long time and are real
quiet, you just might get to see one of those
blue antelope," I said to Cora. "I'd do any-
thing to see a blue antelope," she said. "I'd
take off all my clothes and lie completely still
in the grass all day." "That's a good idea,"
I said, "taking off the clothes, I mean, it's
more natural." I'd met Cora in the library the
night before and had told her about the blue
antelope, so we'd made a date to try and see
them. We lay naked next to one another for hours.
It was a beautiful, sunny day with a breeze that
tickled. Finally, Cora whispered into my ear,
"My God, I see them. They're so delicate, so
graceful. They're like angels, cornflower
angels." I looked at Cora. She was disappearing.
She was becoming one of them.

Read the Great Poets

What good is life without music.
But that's impossible,
one shuffle has always led to another.
One man hears it start on his lathe,
a mother beats her eggs.
There's a typewriter in the next room.
Two cars are angry at each other.
The baby downstairs is wet again.
I remember the voice of a dead friend.
Everything speaks at the same time.
Music will watch us drown.

I write letters to all those from whom I receive
and to many of those from whom I don't.
I read books, anything, useless piles of random
insufferable rubbish for which, in my torpid panic,
I fall through time and space each day
in my foolish way, remembering only the present feeling,
not the village with its face of death,

nothing to be carried secretly in a car.
I move from the stiff-backed chair
to the brown leather one
as the day wears on. And then finally
the couch, allowing the spirit to leave
the broken body and wander at will.
Lately it's a pasture of Holsteins she longs for.

There's a certain point in each evening when I have to put on some really soul-shattering rock-and-roll music and comb my hair into this special caveman fright-wig. I've done as much as two or even three dollars' worth of damage to my apartment in one hour of all-stops-pulled Bacchic, Dionysian celebration and revolution of this great dull life, so fascinating it hypnotizes you and then puts you to sleep, only to never know the ending. It's strange though, no one ever complains. Is it what I feared all along? We are playing the same song and no one has ever heard anything.

People read poems like newspapers, look at paintings as though they were excavations in the City Center, listen to music as if it were rush hour condensed. They don't even know who's invaded whom, what's going to be built there (when, if ever). They get home. That's all that matters to them. They get home. They get home alive.

So what it's been burgled. The heirlooms. Mother's rings, father's cufflinks. They go to a distant island and get robbed there. It's the same everywhere. Read the great poets, listen to the great composers. It's the same everywhere. The Masters. The Thieves.

How the Pope Is Chosen

Any poodle under ten inches high is a toy.
Almost always a toy is an imitation
of something grown-ups use.
Popes with unclipped hair are called *corded popes*.
If a Pope's hair is allowed to grow unchecked,
it becomes extremely long and twists
into long strands that look like ropes.
When it is shorter it is tightly curled.
Popes are very intelligent.
There are three different sizes.
The largest are called standard Popes.
The medium-sized ones are called miniature Popes.
I could go on like this, I could say:
"He is a squarely built Pope, neat,
well-proportioned, with an alert stance
and an expression of bright curiosity,"
but I won't. After a poodle dies
all the cardinals flock to the nearest 7-Eleven.
They drink Slurpees until one of them throws up
and then he's the new Pope.

He is then fully armed and rides through the wilderness alone,
day and night in all kinds of weather.

The new Pope chooses the name he will use as Pope,
like "Wild Bill" or "Buffalo Bill."

He wears red shoes with a cross embroidered on the front.

Most Popes are called "Babe" because
growing up to become a Pope is a lot of fun.

All the time their bodies are becoming bigger and stranger,
but sometimes things happen to make them unhappy.

They have to go to the bathroom by themselves,
and they spend almost all of their time sleeping.

Parents seem to be incapable of helping their little popes grow up.

Fathers tell them over and over again not to lean out of windows,
but the sky is full of them.

It looks as if they are just taking it easy,
but they are learning something else.

What, we don't know, because we are not like them.

We can't even dress like them.

We are like red bugs or mites compared to them.

We think we are having a good time cutting cartoons out of the paper,
but really we are eating crumbs out of their hands.

We are tiny germs that cannot be seen under microscopes.

When a Pope is ready to come into the world,

we try to sing a song, but the words do not fit the music too well.
Some of the full-bodied popes are a million times bigger than us.
They open their mouths at regular intervals.
They are continually grinding up pieces of the cross
and spitting them out. Black flies cling to their lips.
Once they are elected they are given a bowl of cream
and a puppy clip. Eyebrows are a protection
when the Pope must plunge through dense underbrush
in search of a sheep.

The Rules

A man came into the store and said, "I'd like to
have two steaks, about ten ounces each, a half-an-inch
thick, please." I said, "Sir, this is a candy store.
We don't have steaks." He said, "And I'd like to have
two potatoes and a bunch of asparagus." I said, "I'm
sorry, this is a candy store, sir. That's all we carry."
He said, "I don't mind waiting." "It could be many years,"
I said. "I have plenty of time," he said. And, while he
was waiting, a woman came in and said, "Where is your hat
section? I'm hoping you have a large, red hat with a feather."
"I'm awfully sorry, but this is a candy store," I said. "We
don't carry hats." "I'd like to see it, nonetheless," she
said. "It might just fit me." "We only carry candy," I
said. "It might just fit me, anyway," she said. "If you'd
like to wear a piece of candy on your head, I could possibly
find something in red," I said. "That would be lovely,"
she said. And, then, another man came in and pulled out
a gun. "Give me all your money," he said. I said, "I'm
sorry, this is a candy store. We don't do hold ups."
"But I have a gun," he said. "Yes, I can see that, sir,

but it doesn't work in here. This is a candy store," I
said. He looked at the man and woman standing in the corner.
"What about them, can I hold them up?" he said. "Oh no,
I'm afraid not. They're covered under the candy store
protection plan, even though, technically, they don't know
they're in a candy store," I said. "Well, at least I knew
you were a candy store, I just didn't know there were all
these special rules. Can I at least have some jellybeans?
I'll pay you for them, don't worry," he said. As I was getting
him his jellybeans, another man walked in with a gun. "This
is a stickup," he said. "Give me all of your cash." The
first thief said, "This is a candy store, you fool. They
don't do stickups." "What do you mean, they don't do stickups?"
the second thief said. "It's against the rules," the first
one said. "I never read the rule book. I didn't even know
there was one," the second one said. "Would you like some
chocolate kisses, or perhaps some peanut brittle?" I said,
hoping to avert a squabble. He replaced the gun into his
shoulder holster and scanned the glass cases thoughtfully.
"A half-dozen chocolate-covered cherries would make me
a very happy man," he said. "That's what candy stores are
for," I said. The two thieves left together, munching their
candy and chatting about a mutual friend. And that's when
Bonita Sennot and Halissa Delphin came in. Halissa was
wearing a large, red hat with a feather in it. The woman
in the corner leapt forward. "That's it! That's the very
hat I want," she said, yanking the hat off Halissa's head.

Halissa grabbed the lady's arm and threw her to the floor, retrieving her hat. Bonita ordered a bag of malted milk balls. The man in the corner helped the woman to her feet. "That's my hat," she whispered to him. "She's wearing my hat." Halissa invited me to have dinner with them. I said, "Great!"

My Felisberto

My felisberto is handsomer than your mergotroid,
although, admittedly, your mergotroid may be the wiser of the two.
Whereas your mergotroid never winces or quails,
my felisberto is a titan of inconsistencies.
For a night of wit and danger and temptation
my felisberto would be the obvious choice.
However, at dawn or dusk when serenity is desired
your mergotroid cannot be ignored.
Merely to sit near it in the garden
and watch the fabrications of the world swirl by,
the deep-sea's bathymetry wash your eyes,
not to mention the little fawns of the forest
and their flip-floppy gymnastics, ah, for this
and so much more your mergotroid is infinitely preferable.
But there is a place for darkness and obscurity
without which life can sometimes seem too much,
too frivolous and too profound simultaneously,
and that is when my felisberto is needed,

is longed for and loved, and then the sun can rise again.
The bee and the hummingbird drink of the world,
and your mergotroid elaborates the silent concert
that is always and always about to begin.

Neighbors

Will they have children? Will they have more children?
Exactly what is their position on dogs? Large or small?
Chained or running free? Is the wife smarter than the man?
Is she older? Will this cause problems down the line?
Will he be promoted? If not, will this cause marital stress?
Does his family approve of her, and vice versa? How do
they handle the whole in-law situation? Is it causing some
discord already? If she goes back to work, can he fix
his own dinner? Is his endless working about the yard
and puttering with rain gutters really just a pretext
for avoiding the problems inside the house? Do they still
have sex? Do they satisfy one another? Would he like to
have more, would she? Can they talk about their problems?
In their most private fantasies, how would each of them
change their lives? And what do they think of us, as neighbors,
as people? They are certainly cordial to us, painfully
polite when we chance-encounter one another at the roadside
mailboxes—but then, like opposite magnets, we lunge backward,
back into our own deep root systems, darkness and lust

strangling any living thing to quench our thirst and nourish our helplessly solitary lives. And we love our neighborhood for giving us this precious opportunity, and we love our dogs, our children, our husbands and wives. It's just all so damned difficult!

The Painter of the Night

Someone called in a report that she had
seen a man painting in the dark over by the
pond. A police car was dispatched to go in-
vestigate. The two officers with their big
flashlights walked all around the pond, but
found nothing suspicious. Hatcher was the
younger of the two, and he said to Johnson,
"What do you think he was painting?" Johnson
looked bemused and said, "The dark, stupid.
What else could he have been painting?" Hatcher,
a little hurt, said, "Frogs in the Dark, Lily
pads in the Dark, Pond in the Dark. Just as
many things exist in the dark as they do in
the light." Johnson paused, exasperated. Then
Hatcher added, "I'd like to see them. Hell,
I might even buy one. Maybe there's more out
there than we know. We are the police, after
all. We need to know."

The Cowboy

Someone had spread an elaborate rumor about me, that I was
in possession of an extraterrestrial being, and I thought I knew who
it was. It was Roger Lawson. Roger was a practical joker of the
worst sort, and up till now I had not been one of his victims, so
I kind of knew my time had come. People parked in front of my
house for hours and took pictures. I had to draw all my blinds
and only went out when I had to. Then there was a barrage of
questions. "What does he look like?" "What do you feed him?" "How
did you capture him?" And I simply denied the presence of an
extraterrestrial in my house. And, of course, this excited them
all the more. The press showed up and started creeping around
my yard. It got to be very irritating. More and more came and
parked up and down the street. Roger was really working overtime
on this one. I had to do something. Finally, I made an announcement.
I said, "The little fellow died peacefully in his sleep at 11:02
last night." "Let us see the body," they clamored. "He went up
in smoke instantly," I said. "I don't believe you," one of them
said. "There is no body in the house or I would have buried it
myself," I said. About half of them got in their cars and drove

off. The rest of them kept their vigil, but more solemnly now. I went out and bought some groceries. When I came back about an hour later another half of them had gone. When I went into the kitchen I nearly dropped the groceries. There was a nearly transparent fellow with large pink eyes standing about three feet tall. "Why did you tell them I was dead? That was a lie," he said. "You speak English," I said. "I listen to the radio. It wasn't very hard to learn. Also we have television. We get all your channels. I like cowboys, especially John Ford movies. They're the best," he said. "What am I going to do with you?" I said. "Take me to meet a real cowboy. That would make me happy," he said. "I don't know any real cowboys, but maybe we could find one. But people will go crazy if they see you. We'd have press following us everywhere. It would be the story of the century," I said. "I can be invisible. It's not hard for me to do," he said. "I'll think about it. Wyoming or Montana would be our best bet, but they're a long way from here," I said. "Please, I won't cause you any trouble," he said. "It would take some planning," I said. I put the groceries down and started putting them away. I tried not to think of the cosmic meaning of all this. Instead, I treated him like a smart little kid. "Do you have any sarsaparilla?" he said. "No, but I have some orange juice. It's good for you," I said. He drank it and made a face. "I'm going to get the maps out," I said. "We'll see how we could get there." When I came back he was dancing on the kitchen table, a sort of ballet, but very sad. "I have the maps," I said. "We won't need them. I just received word. I'm going to die tonight. It's really a joyous occasion, and I hope you'll help me celebrate by watching *The*

Magnificent Seven," he said. I stood there with the maps in my hand. I felt an unbearable sadness come over me. "Why must you die?" I said. "Father decides these things. It is probably my reward for coming here safely and meeting you," he said. "But I was going to take you to meet a real cowboy," I said. "Let's pretend you are my cowboy," he said.

Worshipful Company of Fletchers

I visited the little boy
at the edge of the woods.
It's still not clear to me
where he really lives.
He'd live with animals
if they'd take him in,
and there would never be
a need to speak. "Who knows,
when you grow up you may be
President," I said, trying
to break the spell.
He flinched as though struck.
"Perhaps something in the field
of numismatics," I continued,
"would be less stressful.
A correspondence school course.
No need to leave the home,
no wretched professor thwacking
your knuckles. In no time
you could hang out your shingle—

STAMPS AND COINS. No more than
one customer per week,
I feel fairly certain: some nerd
who can barely talk—
I'm certainly not speaking of
yourself here—browsing
the liberty dimes and Indian head
pennies, if you see what I mean."
I had meant to comfort him,
but the feral child was now
mewling, and this annoyed me.
"I doubt you have what it takes—
discipline, fastidiousness,
honesty, devotion—to serve
as a manservant, a butler,
to a gentleman of rank and
high-calling. No, I'm afraid
no amount of training
could instill those virtues
into one such as you."
I paused to let the acid burn.
The doe-eyed lad wiped his nose
on his tee-shirt and peeked over
his shoulder into the woods
which seemed to beckon him.
A breeze rustled the leaves
above our heads, and the boy swayed.
A pileated woodpecker tapped

some Morse code into a dead oak tree.
At last, the boy said, "You regret
everything, I bet. You came here
with a crude notion of righting
all that was wrong with your own
bitter childhood, but you have become
your own father—cruel, taunting—
who had become his father, and so on.
It's such a common story.
I wish I could say to you:
'You'd make a fine shepherd,'
but you wouldn't. Your tireless needs
would consume you the first night."
And, with that, the boy stepped forward
and kissed me on the cheek.

I Am a Finn

I am standing in the post office, about
to mail a package back to Minnesota, to my family.
I am a Finn. My name is Kasteheimi (Dewdrop).

Mikael Agricola (1510–1557) created the Finnish language.
He knew Luther and translated the New Testament.
When I stop by the Classé Café for a cheeseburger

no one suspects that I am a Finn.
I gaze at the dime-store reproductions of Lautrec
on the greasy walls, at the punk lovers afraid

to show their quivery emotions, secure
in the knowledge that my grandparents really did
emigrate from Finland in 1910—why

is everyone leaving Finland, hundreds of
thousands to Michigan and Minnesota, and now Australia?
Eighty-six percent of Finnish men have blue

or gray eyes. Today is Charlie Chaplin's
one hundredth birthday, though he is not
Finnish or alive: "Thy blossom, in the bud

laid low." The commonest fur-bearing animals
are the red squirrel, muskrat, pine-marten
and fox. There are about 35,000 elk.

But I should be studying for my exam.
I wonder if Dean will celebrate with me tonight,
assuming I pass. Finnish literature

really came alive in the 1860s.
Here, in Cambridge, Massachusetts,
no one cares that I am a Finn.

They've never even heard of Frans Eemil Sillanpää,
winner of the 1939 Nobel Prize in Literature.
As a Finn, this infuriates me.

I Am Still a Finn

I failed my exam, which is difficult
for me to understand because I am a Finn.
We are a bright, if slightly depressed, people.

Pertti Palmroth is the strongest name
in Finnish footwear design; his shoes and boots
are exported to seventeen countries.

Dean brought champagne to celebrate
my failure. He says I was just nervous.
Between 1908 and 1950, 33 volumes

of The Ancient Poetry of the Finnish People
were issued, the largest work of its kind
ever published in any language.

So why should I be nervous? Aren't I
a Finn, descendant of Johan Ludvig Runeberg
(1804–1877), Finnish National poet?

I know he wrote in Swedish, and this
depresses me still. Harvard Square
is never "empty." There is no chance

that I will ever be able to state honestly
that "Harvard Square is empty tonight."
A man from Nigeria will be opening

his umbrella, and a girl from Wyoming
will be closing hers. A Zulu warrior
is running to catch a bus and an over-

painted harlot from Buenos Aires will
be fainting on schedule. And I, a Finn,
will long for the dwarf birches of the north

I have never seen. For 73 days the sun
never sinks below the horizon. O
darkness, mine! I shall always be a Finn.

The Formal Invitation

I was invited to a formal dinner party given by Marguerite Farnish
Burridge and her husband, Knelm Oswald Lancelot Burridge. I
had never met either of them, and had no idea why I was invited.
When the butler announced me, Mrs. Burridge came up and greeted me
quite graciously. "I'm so happy you could join us," she said.
"I know Knelm is looking forward to talking to you later." "I
can't wait," I said, "I mean, the pleasure's all mine." Nothing
came out right. I wanted to escape right then, but Mrs. Burridge
dragged me and introduced me to some of her friends. "This is
Nicholas and Sondra Pepperdene. Nicholas is a spy," she said.
"I am not," he said. "Yes, you are, darling. Everyone knows it,"
she said. "And Sondra does something with swans, I'm not
sure what. She probably mates them, knowing Sondra." "Really!
I'm saving them from extinction," Mrs. Pepperdene said. "And this
is Mordecai Rhinelander, and, as you might guess from his name,
he's a Nazi. And his wife, Dagmar, is a Nazi, too. Still, lovely
people," she said. "Marguerite, you're giving our new friend
a very bad impression," Mr. Rhinelander said. "Oh, it's my party
and I can say what I want," Mrs. Burridge said. A servant was
passing with cocktails and she grabbed two off the tray and handed

me one. "I hope you like martinis," she said, and left me standing there. "My name is Theodore Fullerton," I said, "and I'm a depraved jazz musician. I prey on young women, take drugs whenever possible, but most of the time I just sleep all day and am out of work." They looked at one another, and then broke out laughing. I smiled like an idiot and sipped my drink. I thought it was going to be an awful party, but I just told the truth whenever I was spoken to, and people thought I was hilariously funny. At dinner, I was seated between Carmen Milanca and Godina Barnafi. The first course was fresh crabmeat on a slice of kiwi. Mine managed to slip off the plate and landed in the lap of Carmen Milanca. She had on a very tight, short black dress. She smiled at me, waiting to see what I would do. I reached over and plucked it from its nest. "Nice shot," she said. "It was something of a bull's-eye, wasn't it?" I said. Godina Barnafi asked me if I found wealthy women to be sexy. "Oh yes, of course," I said, "but I generally prefer poor, homeless waifs, you know, runaways, mentally addled, unwashed, sickly, starving women." "Fascinating," she said. A leg of lamb was served. Knelm Burridge proposed a toast. "To my good friends gathered here tonight, and to your great achievements in the further-ance of peace on Earth." I still had no idea what I was doing there. I mentioned this to Carmen since we'd almost been intimate. "You're probably the sacrificial lamb," she said. "The what?" I said. "The human sacrifice, you know, to the gods, for peace," she said. "I figure it's got to be you, because I recognize all the rest of them, and they're friends." "You've got to be kidding me," I said. "No, we all work for peace in our various ways, and then once a year we get together and have this dinner." "But why me?" I said. "That's Marguerite's job. She does the research all year, and she tries to pick someone who won't be missed, someone who's not giving in a positive way to society, someone who is essentially selfish. Her choices are very carefully considered and fair, I think, though I am sorry it's you this time. I think I could get to like you," she said. I picked at my food. "Well, I guess I was a rather good choice, except that some people really like my music. They even say it heals them," I said. "I'm sure it does," Carmen said, "but Marguerite takes everything into consideration. She's very thorough."

Uneasy about the Sounds of Some Night-Wandering Animal

On the way to work this morning, the newsman on the radio said, "A big part of reality has been removed, it has been reported. Details are not available at this time. It's just that, I am told, you will find things different on your drive to work this morning. Some roads will be missing, whole areas of the city may be gone. However, the good news is, no signs of violence have been detected." I turned the radio off. There wasn't the usual rush hour traffic, for which I was grateful. I wasn't even sure I was on the right road. There were empty fields where I had remembered rows and rows of apartment buildings. Then I went into a long tunnel, and I had no memory of there being a tunnel. When I came out of it, there was nothing, or, rather, I guess it was a desert, as I had never been in the desert before. I looked around for signs of the city. A jackrabbit scurried across the road, and up ahead a policeman was leaning against his motorcycle. I slowed down instinctively, and then pulled over to stop. "Good morning, officer," I said. "I seem to have taken a wrong turn. Could you tell me where I

am?" "Not exactly," he said. "This seems to be a new area.
It wasn't here before. We're still trying to identify it.
I suggest you drive with caution, because, well, we have no infor-
mation on it as yet." I noticed that he was about to cry. "Well,
thanks," I said. My stomach was sinking. I was certain to be
late to work. I didn't know what to do. Part of me wanted to
drive on, to see what was out there, and part of me wanted to
turn back, though I wasn't certain of what I would find there.
So I drove on for miles and miles, the sand dunes shifting and
stirring, and the occasional hawk or buzzard circling overhead.
Then the road disappeared, and I was forced to stop, and looked
behind me, but that road, too, was gone, blown over by sand in
a few seconds. I got out of the car, glad that I had some water
with me. I looked around, and it was all the same. Nothing made
any sense. I tried to call Harvey at the office on my cell phone.
I couldn't believe when he answered. "Harvey, it's Carl. I'm
out here in this new place. It's all sand, and there are no roads,"
I said. "We'll come get you," he said. "But I don't know where
I am, I mean, I don't even know if it exists," I said. "Don't
be ridiculous, Carl, of course it exists. Just look around and
give me something to go by," he said. "There's nothing here.
Oh, there was a tunnel some miles back, and a policeman leaning up
against his motorcycle. That's the last thing I saw," I said.
"Was it the old Larchmont tunnel?" he said. "I don't know, it could
have been. I was lost already," I said. "Okay, I'm going to
come get you. Just stay put," he said. I waited and waited. And
then I just started walking. I know I wasn't supposed to, but
I was restless and hoped I might find a way out. I had lost

sight of my car and had no idea where I was. The sun was blinding
me and I couldn't think straight. I barely knew who I was.
And, then, as if by miracle, I heard Harvey's voice call my name.
I looked around and couldn't see him. "Carl, Carl, I'm here,"
he said. And I still couldn't see him. "We've fallen off. We're
in the fallen off zone," he said. "What? What does that mean?"
I said. "We've separated. It may be temporary. It's too soon
to tell," he said. "But where are we. We must be in some relation
to something," I said. "I think we're parallel," he said. "Parallel
to what?" I said. "Parallel to everything that matters," he said.
"Then that's good," I said. I still couldn't see him, and night
was coming on. It was a parallel night, much like the other,
and that was some comfort, cold comfort, as they like to say.

Dear Reader

I am trying to pry open your casket
with this burning snowflake.

I'll give up my sleep for you.
This freezing sleet keeps coming down
and I can barely see.

If this trick works we can rub our hands
together, maybe

start a little fire
with our identification papers.
I don't know but I keep working, working

half hating you,
half eaten by the moon.

I Left My Couch in Tatamagouche

I desired lemonade—
It was hot and I had been walking for hours—
but after much wrestling,
pushing and shoving,
I simply could not get my couch
through the restaurant door.
Several customers and the owner
and the owner's son
were kinder than they should have been,
but finally it was time to close
and I urged them to return to their homes,
their families needed them
(the question of who needs what
was hardly my field of expertise).
That night, while sleeping peacefully
outside the train station
on my little, green couch,
I met a giantess by the name of Anna Swan.
She knelt beside my couch

and stroked my brow with tenderness.
She was like a mother to me
for a few moments there under the night sky.
In the morning, I left my couch in Tatamagouche,
and that has made a big difference.

My Great Great Etc. Uncle Patrick Henry

There's a fortune to be made in just about everything
in this country, somebody's father had to invent
everything—baby food, tractors, rat poisoning.
My family's obviously done nothing since the beginning
of time. They invented poverty and bad taste
and getting by and taking it from the boss.
O my mother goes around chewing her nails and
spitting them in a jar: You should be ashamed
of yourself she says, think of your family.
My family I say what have they ever done but
paint by numbers the most absurd disgusting scenes
of plastic squalor and human degradation.
Well then think of your great great etc. Uncle
Patrick Henry.

Teaching the Ape to Write Poems

They didn't have much trouble
teaching the ape to write poems:
first they strapped him into the chair,
then tied the pencil around his hand
(the paper had already been nailed down).
Then Dr. Bluespire leaned over his shoulder
And whispered into his ear:
"You look like a god sitting there.
Why don't you try writing something?"

The List of Famous Hats

Napoleon's hat is an obvious choice I guess to list as a famous hat, but that's not the hat I have in mind. That was his hat for show. I am thinking of his private bathing cap, which in all honesty wasn't much different than the one any jerk might buy at a corner drugstore now, except for two minor eccentricities. The first one isn't even funny: Simply it was a white rubber bathing cap, but too small. Napoleon led such a hectic life ever since his childhood, even farther back than that, that he never had a chance to buy a new bathing cap and still as a grown-up—well, he didn't really grow that much, but his head did: He was a pinhead at birth, and he used, until his death really, the same little tiny bathing cap that he was born in, and this meant that later it was very painful to him and gave him many headaches, as if he needed more. So, he had to vaseline his skull like crazy to even get the thing on. The second eccentricity was that it was a tricorn bathing cap. Scholars like to make a lot out of this, and it would be easy to do. My theory is simple-minded to be sure: that beneath his public head there was another head and it was a pyramid or something.

Distance from Loved Ones

After her husband died, Zita decided to get the face-lift
she had always wanted. Halfway through the operation
her blood pressure started to drop, and they had to stop.
When Zita tried to fasten her seat belt for her sad drive
home, she threw out her shoulder. Back at the hospital
the doctor examined her and found cancer run rampant
throughout her shoulder and arm and elsewhere. Radiation
followed. And, now, Zita just sits there in her beauty parlor,
bald, crying and crying.

My mother tells me all this on the phone, and I say:
Mother, who is Zita?

And my mother says, I am Zita. All my life I have been
Zita, bald and crying. And you, my son, who should have known
me best, thought I was nothing but your mother.

But, Mother, I say, I am dying. . . .

Go, Youth

I was in a dream state and this was causing a problem
with the traffic. I felt lonely, like I'd missed the boat,
or I'd found the boat and it was deserted. In the middle
of the road a child's shoe glistened. I walked around it.
It woke me up a little. The child had disappeared. Some
mysteries are better left alone. Others are dreary, distasteful,
and can disarrange a shadow into a thing of unspeakable beauty.
Whose child is that?

Loyalty

This is the hardest part:
when I came back to life
I was a good family dog
and not too friendly to strangers.
I got a thirty-five dollar raise
in salary, and through the pea-soup fogs
I drove the General, and introduced him
at rallies. I had a totalitarian approach
and was a massive boost to his popularity.
I did my best to reduce the number of people.
The local bourgeoisie did not exist.
One of them was a mystic
and walked right over me
as if I were a bed of hot coals.
This is par for the course—
I will be employing sundry golf metaphors
henceforth, because a dog, best friend
and chief advisor to the General, should.
While dining with the General I said,
"Let's play the back nine in a sacred rage.

Let's tee-off over the foredoomed community
and putt ourselves thunderously, touching bottom."
He drank it all in, rugged and dusky.
I think I know what he was thinking.
He held his automatic to my little head
and recited a poem about my many weaknesses,
for which I loved him so.

Where Babies Come From

Many are from the Maldives,
southwest of India, and must begin
collecting shells almost immediately.
The larger ones may prefer coconuts.
Survivors move from island to island
hopping over one another and never
looking back. After the typhoons
have had their pick, and the birds of prey
have finished with theirs, the remaining few
must build boats, and in this, of course,
they can have no experience, they build
their boats of palm leaves and vines.
Once the work is completed, they lie down,
thoroughly exhausted and confused,
and a huge wave washes them out to sea.
And that is the last they see of one another.
In their dreams Mama and Papa
are standing on the shore
for what seems like an eternity,
and it is almost always the wrong shore.

Never Again the Same

Speaking of sunsets,
last night's was shocking.
I mean, sunsets aren't supposed to frighten you, are they?
Well, this one was terrifying.
People were screaming in the streets.
Sure, it was beautiful, but far too beautiful.
It wasn't natural.
One climax followed another and then another
until your knees went weak
and you couldn't breathe.
The colors were definitely not of this world,
peaches dripping opium,
pandemonium of tangerines,
inferno of irises,
Plutonian emeralds,
all swirling and churning, swabbing,
like it was playing with us,
like we were nothing,
as if our whole lives were a preparation for this,
this for which nothing could have prepared us

and for which we could not have been less prepared.
The mockery of it all stung us bitterly.
And when it was finally over
we whimpered and cried and howled.
And then the streetlights came on as always
and we looked into one another's eyes—
ancient caves with still pools
and those little transparent fish
who have never seen even one ray of light.
And the calm that returned to us
was not even our own.

Toads Talking by a River

A book can move from room to room
without anyone touching it. It can climb
the staircase and hide under the bed. It
can crawl into bed with you because it knows
you need company. And it can read to you
in your sleep and you wake a smarter person
or a sadder person. It is good to live
surrounded by books because you never know
what can happen next: lost in the inter-
stellar space between teacups in the cupboard,
found in the beak of a downy woodpecker,
the lovers staring into the void and then
jumping over it, flying into their beautiful
tomorrows like the heroes of a storm.

Torture

Eleanor goes to see her psychiatrist
twice a week. Whatever she tells him he
invariably tells her that it is normal to feel
that way. She tells him that she wants to
kill herself and he says everybody does.
She tells him she wants to make love in
a crowded restaurant and he says of course
that is a perfectly normal thing to want.
She tells him most days she can't get out
of bed and she can't stop crying for hours
at a time. He says that's the basic human
condition. Before her decline into this
maelstrom she was a loving, caring person
with many friends and interests. Now it
seems the doctor has convinced her that
everyone is just like her so why bother,
they're jerks, and she alone stars in the
drama of the century: ELEANOR, Ruthless
Conqueror of the Dark Ages.

The Bookclub

Bobbie came home from her bookclub
completely drunk and disheveled. Three
buttons from her blouse were missing and
she had scratches down both cheeks. "Jesus,"
I said, "what the hell happened to you?"
"They all hated that book," she said, "you
know, that one that had me crying all last
week, about the girl's mother dying, and
then her baby getting sick and her husband
leaving her. They said it was corny, and
I just couldn't take it. I couldn't sit
there and make fun of that poor
woman." "So what happened?" I said. "Well,
Irene was laughing and that's when I got up
and slapped her. And she punched me in the
gut and I grabbed her hair and threw her to
the floor and kicked her in the face. And
then Rosie and Tina and that bitch Sonia
from Leverett all jumped on me and punched
me a hundred times and I didn't know what

was happening." "So when did you get drunk?"
I asked. "Oh, when it was all over we went
out to Lucky 7 together and laughed and
laughed about it." "A bunch of tough broads,"
I said. "Nah, they're all pussycats," she
said, looking badly in need of repair.

Of Whom Am I Afraid?

I was feeling a little at loose ends, so
I went to the Farmer's Supply store and just
strolled up and down the aisles, examining
the merchandise, none of which was of any use
to me, but the feed sacks and seeds had a calm-
ing effect on me. At some point there was an
old, grizzled farmer standing next to me holding
a rake, and I said to him, "Have you ever read
much Emily Dickinson?" "Sure," he said, "I
reckon I've read all of her poems at least a
dozen times. She's a real pistol. And I've
even gotten into several fights about them
with some of my neighbors. One guy said she
was too 'prissy' for him. And I said, 'Hell,
she's tougher than you'll ever be.' When I
finished with him, I made him sit down and read
The Complete Poems over again, all 1,775 of them.
He finally said, 'You're right, Clyde, she's
tougher than I'll ever be.' And he was crying

like a baby when he said that." Clyde slapped
my cheek and headed toward the counter with
his new rake. I bought some ice tongs, which
made me surprisingly happy, and for which I
had no earthly use.

A Largely Questioning Article Offering Few Answers

When Roberta came home from the hospital she had tears
in her eyes. I grabbed her and kissed her. "What happened?"
I said. "He died," she said. "Who died?" I said. "The doctor.
When he entered Mother's room he was so startled he had a
heart attack," she said. "I don't understand. What startled him?"
I said. "Mother. She had grown nine feet tall, and her
face is all contorted. She's really quite frightening," she
said. "Isn't there anything they can do for her?" I said.
"All the medicines they have given her are tearing her apart.
They are anxious for her to die, but she seems to just keep
getting stronger. They are at an utter loss of what to do next,"
she said. "Perhaps we should take her out of there," I said.
"But she wouldn't really fit in this house, or any house I can
think of," she said. "Perhaps we should just take her out into
the wild and let her go," I said. Roberta went silent and started
fidgeting about the kitchen. She put away dishes and mopped
the counter. I said, "Roberta?" And she said, "I'm thinking."
She put out fresh mouse poison beneath the sink, something I'd
never seen her do. We drove to the hospital and checked her
mother out. They were only too glad to see us go. We stuffed

her mother into the backseat, which was quite an ordeal. She had to lie down and then we stuffed her legs practically up to her chin. Her mother was screaming and kicking at us. We drove out of town to a wilderness area where I had hiked years ago. We drove in on a little bumpy road until we could hear nothing but the running of a creek. I stopped the car. Roberta and I looked at each other. Her mother was screaming all the time. We got out and opened the back door. Her mother kicked me so hard I stumbled backward and fell. Then she got out of the car by herself and roared. Rocks tumbled and trees fell. I crawled to my feet, cowering. Roberta shouted, "Mother, I love you!" "Hmmpf!" her mother replied. "There is never enough love." "We'll visit you," Roberta said. "I'll bet you will," her mother said, marching off into the darkening hills. "Do you think she'll be all right?" Roberta said. "She's at the very top of the food chain. It gets lonely up there," I said.

The Rules

Jack told me to never reveal my true identity. "I would
never do that," I said. "Always wear at least a partial disguise,"
he said. "Of course," I said. "And try to blend in with the
crowd," he said. "Naturally," I said. "And never fall in love,"
he said. "Far too dangerous," I said. "Never raise your voice,"
he said. "Understood," I said. "Never run," he said. "I
wouldn't dream of it," I said. "Never make a glutton of yourself,"
he said. "It won't happen," I said. "Always be polite," he
said. "That's me, polite," I said. "Don't sing in public,"
he said. "You have my promise," I said. "Don't touch strangers,"
he said. "That's forbidden," I said. "Never speed," he said.
"You can count on me," I said. "Don't wear plaid," he said.
"No plaid," I said. "Don't pet dogs," he said. "Of course
not," I said. "Don't jump fences," he said. "I won't," I
said. "Stay away from children," he said. "I will," I said.
"Don't enter churches," he said. "Of course not," I said.
"Good posture at all times," he said. "Good posture is a must,"
I said. "Never pick money out of the gutter," he said. "That's
not for me," I said. "Be punctual," he said. "Always on time,"
I said. "When walking or driving always mix your routes," he

said. "Naturally," I said. "Never order the same meal twice," he said. "Never," I said. "Do not be seen on the street after midnight," he said. "Not ever," I said. "Do not give money to homeless beggars," he said. "Nothing for the beggars," I said. "Do not start conversations with officers of the law," he said. "No talking with cops," I said. "No ice skating," he said. "Never," I said. "No skiing," he said. "Of course not," I said. "When a sign says STAY OFF THE GRASS, you'll stay off," he said. "I will," I said. "No chewing gum in public," he said. "I won't," I said. "You must carry your weapon at all times," he said. "Always armed," I said. "You must follow orders," he said. "Count on it," I said. "You will contact Central once a week," he said. "Contact Central," I said. "No green pants," he said. "Certainly not," I said. "No orange or purple shirts," he said. "Not for me," I said. "No sushi," he said. "Oh no," I said. "No fandango," he said. "Not possible," I said. "No farm bureau," he said. "Not my style," I said. "Beware hypnotism," he said. "Always alert," I said. "Watch out for leeches," he said. "A danger not forgotten," I said. "Stay off gondolas." "Instinctively," I said. "Never trust a fortune-teller," he said. "Never," I said. "Avoid crusades," he said. "Certainly," I said. "Never ride on a blimp," he said. "Blimps are out," I said. "Do not chase turkeys," he said. "I will not," I said. "Do not put your hand in the mouth of a horse," he said. "Out of the question," I said. "Never believe in miracles," he said. "I won't," I said.

Roscoe's Farewell

The dog played in the snow all afternoon. When we called it in, it was shivering, and it took hours of warm towel rubbings before it settled down. Then it slept like a baby. When it didn't get up in the morning we were worried. Finally my mother went to take its temperature and that's when we realized it was dead. We were all so sad we didn't know what to do. Dad said we should bury it in the backyard, with a full ceremony. So we dug a hole and decided on some scripture to read. Janet picked out some music to play. The next morning we went out to look at the grave and it was all torn up and Roscoe was gone. There were footprints in the snow, so we followed them. They went on for several blocks until we found him playing by a lake with several other dogs. He wouldn't come when we called him. We had to chase him and tackle him before we could lead him home. When we got him in the house he was sweet as ever. We fed him and he cozied up on the couch next to us. We still didn't know how we could have mistaken him for dead. Weeks went by as normal. Then, just as spring was coming on, Roscoe was hit by a car right in front of our house. This time we were sure he was dead and buried him in the previous hole we had not filled in. This time without scripture or music. We just threw him in and covered it up with the old dirt. A week went by and then one day in the schoolyard at recess, there he was, as pert and lively as ever before. I called to him and he came to me. I was so glad to see him I didn't know what to do. My parents were happy, too, though a little confused. We welcomed him home, fed him mightily, and played with him as much as he liked. We thought he might live forever. But slowly we forgot about that and he was just Roscoe our old dog whom we took for granted and barely remembered to feed. He fell ill one day and we didn't even call the vet because, I guess, we thought he would live forever. But he didn't. He died a week later and this time we didn't even bother to throw him in the hole, so sure were we that he would come back to life. We just laid him on the back porch and waited for the miracle to happen a third time. Flies gathered and finally he turned to dust. We swept the back porch as we always had before. Roscoe disappeared forever among the flowerpots and old tin cans, saying goodbye to this world one last time.

Shroud of the Gnome

And what amazes me is that none of our modern inventions
surprise or interest him, even a little. I tell him
it is time he got his booster shots, but then
I realize I have no power over him whatsoever.
He becomes increasingly light-footed until I lose sight
of him downtown between the federal building and
the post office. A registered nurse is taking her
coffee break. I myself needed a break, so I sat down
next to her at the counter. "Don't mind me," I said,
"I'm just a hungry little Gnostic in need of a sandwich."
(This old line of mine had met with great success
on any number of previous occasions.) I thought,
a deaf, dumb, and blind nurse, sounds ideal!
But then I remembered that some of the earliest
Paleolithic office workers also feigned blindness
when approached by nonoffice workers, so I paid my bill
and disappeared down an alley where I composed myself.
Amid the piles of outcast citizenry and burning barrels
of waste and rot, the plump rats darting freely,
the havoc of blown newspapers, lay the little shroud

of my lost friend: small and gray and threadbare,
windworn by the ages of scurrying hither and thither,
battered by the avalanches and private tornadoes
of just being a gnome, but surely there were good times, too.
And now, rejuvenated by the wind, the shroud moves forward,
hesitates, dances sideways, brushes my foot as if for a kiss,
and flies upward, whistling a little-known ballad
about the pitiful, raw etiquette of the underworld.

Finding Out Something in a Cafe

Clusters of spoons
clamber from their shelves:
the stiff, wicked rain

has made void my stealth.
So I get intimate
with inferior products;

I marry the thick,
beige crockery,
and dream everlastingly

of a diesel truck
in a wet, wrinkled nightgown.
This ignoble, negligible

vision of myself
is kissing the moral examiner
on the ear and nose,

quivering like a flashlight
in a deep, silent basement.
Do I have the right

to be afraid?
In the adjacent booth,
tiny, pink gods

nod in their sleep.

Suffering Bastards

The blight of poems in our time,
there is no darkness dark enough.
No, there is no darkness the blind
cannot see through, ungraspable
as they are, the suffering bastards
on balconies, in love with a solitary
maggot.

     O semen of Shiva, there is
no voice at the end of the darkness,
no there is no darkness, light
proceeds in brittle nightgowns
with not a word for anyone.

The Rally

There was some kind of rally going on in the
common. Somebody was speaking into a bullhorn to
about three hundred people, who were cheering and
shouting things. I decided to drift over and check
it out. The speaker was saying, "Even my three-year-
old son knows better than to kick a goat." I mingled
with the crowd. A woman yelled, "You got a great big
cherry pie on your head!" And a dozen others said,
"Yes you do." The man continued, "And, then, the dog
ate our sofa. Did we kick it? No we didn't." Someone
shouted, "The saints dropped the ball on that one."
The man said, "I been down there where even the little
birdies fear to roam. I once found an angry viper
in my pocket, but I steered the course. I bonged myself
with a hidden cloud." "And you never lost your way,"
many shrieked. I was working my way toward the front.
The excitement was catching. "If you spit in a burning
skillet, sure, it sizzles, and then it's gone, and what
have you got? You have the memory of the sizzle, but,
soon that, too, is gone, and you're poorer than you were

before," he said. "Your duck just sat on a firecracker,"
I cheered. The speaker stopped and tried to locate
the man who had spoken those words. The crowd, too,
was looking around. I acted as though I were looking
also. After a considerable pause, he continued, "Never
before have we witnessed hairy hands with long fingernails
curl around the puffballs of history with such miraculous
dexterity." The people went crazy. They started bumping
one another's foreheads. I was bumping, and getting
bumped. "It was no accident I swallowed an ant this
morning while preparing my remarks for this rally. I
wanted to swallow that ant," he said. People had stopped
bumping, and now many of them were wiping away tears.
I had to admit, he was a powerful speaker. "And now we
are on the verge of setting sail the little headache and
the big headache, too, and we can see the fireflies, who
had all but forgotten us, beating their wings like idiot
children coming back from a dull day in the park, and
it is beautiful, can't you see just how marvelous it is?"
he said. "We love the idiot children," someone shouted.
"Fireflies can't drive tractors," another yelled. "What
happened to the pig?" I said. The man next to me looked
disgusted. "There is no pig," he said.

Lewis and Clark Overheard in Conversation

then we'll get us some wine and spare ribs
then we'll get us some wine and spare ribs
then we'll get us some wine and spare ribs
then we'll get us some wine and spare ribs
then we'll get us some wine and spare ribs
then we'll get us some wine and spare ribs
then we'll get us some wine and spare ribs
then we'll get us some wine and spare ribs
then we'll get us some wine and spare ribs
then we'll get us some wine and spare ribs
then we'll get us some wine and spare ribs
then we'll get us some wine and spare ribs
then we'll get us some wine and spare ribs
then we'll get us some wine and spare ribs
then we'll get us some wine and spare ribs
then we'll get us some wine and spare ribs
then we'll get us some wine and spare ribs
then we'll get us some wine and spare ribs
then we'll get us some wine and spare ribs
then we'll get us some wine and spare ribs
then we'll get us some wine and spare ribs
then we'll get us some wine and spare ribs

Wild Beasts

In the front all the weapons were
loaded. We sat there in the dark with
not so much as a whisper. We could hear
sounds outside—skirrs, rasps, the occasional
yap, ting. We were alert, perhaps too
alert. Ready to shoot a fly for just
being a fly. When you don't sleep you
start to hallucinate and that's not good.
One night this crazy notion started to
possess me: I said, "Who are our enemies
anyhow? We don't have any enemies. What
are we doing here? We should be with our
families doing what families do. I'm laying
down this gun and I'm leaving right now."
I knew there was a chance that one of them
might shoot me. Instead they all laid down
their guns and we walked right out into the moon-
lit night, frightened, now, only of ourselves.

The Ice Cream Man

I answered the ad in the paper. I had been unemployed for
nine months and was desperate. At the interview, the man said,
"Do you have much experience climbing tall mountains?" "Absolutely.
I climb them all the time. If I see a tall mountain, I have to
climb it immediately," I said. "What about swimming long distances
in rough ocean waters, perhaps in a storm?" he said. "I'm like
a fish, you can't stop me. I just keep going in all kinds of
weather," I said. "Could you fly a glider at night and land in
a wheat field, possibly under enemy fire?" he said. "Nothing
could come more naturally to me," I said. "How are you with
explosives? Would a large building, say, twenty stories high
present you with much difficulty?" he said. "Certainly not. I
pride myself on a certain expertise," I said. "And I take it you
are fully acquainted with the latest in rocket launchers and land-
mines?" he said. "I even own a few myself for personal use. They're
definitely no problem for me," I said. "Now, Mr. Strafford, or may
I call you Stephen, what you'll be doing is driving one of our ice
cream trucks, selling ice cream to all the little kids in the
neighborhood, but sometimes things get tricky and we like all our
drivers to be well-trained and well-equipped to face any eventu-

ality, you know, some fathers can get quite irate if you are out of their kid's favorite flavor or if the kid drops the cone," he said. "I understand, I won't hesitate to take appropriate action," I said. "And there are certain neighborhoods where you're under advisement to expect the worst, sneak attacks, gang tactics, bodies dropping from trees or rising out of manholes, blockades, machine gun fire, launched explosives, flamethrowers and that kind of thing. You can still do a little business there if you are on your toes. Do you see what I'm saying?" he said. "No problem. I know those kinds of neighborhoods, but, as you say, kids still want their ice cream and I won't let them down," I said. "Good, Stephen, I think you're going to like this job. It's exciting and challenging. We've, of course, lost a few drivers over the years, but mostly it was because they weren't paying attention. It's what I call the Santa Claus complex. They thought they were there just to make the kids happy. But there's a lot more to it than that. One of our best drivers had to level half the city once. Of course, that was an extreme case, but he did what needed to be done. We'll count on you to be able to make that kind of decision. You'll have to have all your weapons loaded and ready to go in a moment's notice. You'll have your escape plans with you at all times," he said. "Yes, sir, I'll be ready at all times," I said. "And, as you know, some of the ice cream is lethal, so that will require a quick judgment call on your part as well. Mistakes will inevitably be made, but try to keep them at a minimum, otherwise the front office becomes flooded with paperwork," he said. "I can assure you I will use it only when I deem it absolutely necessary," I said. "Well, Stephen, I look forward to your joining our team. They're mostly crack professionals, ex–Green Berets and Navy Seals and that kind of thing. At the end of the day you've made all those kids happy, but you've also thinned out the bad seeds and made our city a safer place to be," he said. He sat there smiling with immense pride. "How will I know which flavor is lethal?" I said. "Experiment," he said. I looked stunned, then we both started laughing.

The War Next Door

I thought I saw some victims of the last war bandaged and limping through the forest beside my house. I thought I recognized some of them, but I wasn't sure. It was kind of a hazy dream from which I tried to wake myself, but they were still there, bloody, some of them on crutches, some lacking limbs. This sad parade went on for hours. I couldn't leave the window. Finally, I opened the door. "Where are you going?" I shouted. "We're just trying to escape," one of them shouted back. "But the war's over," I said. "No it's not," one said. All the news reports had said it had been over for days. I didn't know who to trust. It's best to just ignore them, I told myself. They'll go away. So I went into the living room and picked up a magazine. There was a picture of a dead man. He had just passed my house. And another dead man I recognized. I ran back in the kitchen and looked out. A group of them were headed my way. I opened the door. "Why didn't you fight with us?" they said. "I didn't know who the enemy was, honest, I didn't," I said. "That's a fine answer. I never did figure it out myself," one of them said. The others looked at him as if he were crazy. "The other side was the enemy, obviously, the ones with the beady eyes," said another. "They were mean," another said, "terrible." "One was very kind to me, cradled me in his arms," said one. "Well, you're all dead now. A lot of good that will do you," I said. "We're just gaining our strength back," one of them said. I shut the door and went back in the living room. I heard scratches at the window at first, but then they faded off. I heard a bugle in the distance, then the roar of a cannon. I still didn't know which side I was on.

Everything But Thomas

I walked out of the bank just as I realized it was being held up.
I didn't know what to do, run or hide in the bushes. So, without thinking,
I turned around and walked back in the bank. The thief saw me and said,
"Get down on the ground!" I followed his instructions and got down on
the floor. Then he pointed to me and said, "You, get up. You're going
with me." I got up and followed him. We got in his car and sped away.
We sped past other cars at first, through stoplights, until we finally came to
a parking lot. We got out of the car and quickly got into another, it was
a black Chevy. Then we took off at a normal speed and drove that way from
then on, stopping at stoplights and obeying all the rules. We drove out
past the city limits and into the countryside. If I didn't know any better I'd
say it was a pretty ride, beautiful trees and quaint little cottages. We
drove for about an hour, then pulled off on a little lane and followed that
for another twenty minutes. Then we stopped by a small cottage and got out.
We walked in and turned on the lights. He said, "Sit down." I did and
he got out a rope and tied me up. Then I watched him go about his business.
He took his gun out of his shoulder holster. He made some coffee, he
lowered the blinds. He was nervous, but he also felt good about how things
went. I also felt strangely secure, though I was a captive and tied up.
He looked at me and said, "What are you thinking?" I said, "I feel pretty

good, considering." "You should. Everything's gone as planned so far," he said. "They don't know who I am and we got away pretty neatly as far as I can tell." "Good. We'll just hunker down here and no one will find us," I said. He went to the stove and started cooking up some hot dogs. He loosened my ropes so I could eat with him. "This is a nice place," I said. "Yeah, it was my grandfather's," he said. After lunch he tied me back up. Then he said, "I'm going to take a nap, alright?" I said, "Sure." And he slept for a couple of hours. After several weeks together he decided to untie me. I helped around the house, chopping wood, sweeping the floors, occasionally cooking something. We were a good couple together. I grew very fond of him. And I know he liked me. This was our home, and neither one of us ever wanted to go back. There was a little grocery store about five miles away, and that was all we needed. We hunted deer and one was all we needed to make it through the winter. Then one day Thomas got sick. He wouldn't let me call a doctor, and a week later he died. To my surprise he left me everything, the money from the bank robbery and the cabin. I stayed on there for the rest of my life, never marrying, never having children. I had everything I wanted, everything I needed, everything but Thomas.

It Happens Like This

I was outside St. Cecilia's Rectory
smoking a cigarette when a goat appeared beside me.
It was mostly black and white, with a little reddish
brown here and there. When I started to walk away,
it followed. I was amused and delighted, but wondered
what the laws were on this kind of thing. There's
a leash law for dogs, but what about goats? People
smiled at me and admired the goat. "It's not my goat,"
I explained. "It's the town's goat. I'm just taking
my turn caring for it." "I didn't know we had a goat,"
one of them said. "I wonder when my turn is." "Soon,"
I said. "Be patient. Your time is coming." The goat
stayed by my side. It stopped when I stopped. It looked
up at me and I stared into its eyes. I felt he knew
everything essential about me. We walked on. A police-
man on his beat looked us over. "That's a mighty
fine goat you got there," he said, stopping to admire.
"It's the town's goat," I said. "His family goes back
three hundred years with us," I said, "from the beginning."
The officer leaned forward to touch him, then stopped

and looked up at me. "Mind if I pat him?" he asked.
"Touching this goat will change your life," I said.
"It's your decision." He thought real hard for a minute,
and then stood up and said, "What's his name?" "He's
called the Prince of Peace," I said. "God! This town
is like a fairy tale. Everywhere you turn there's mystery
and wonder. And I'm just a child playing cops and robbers
forever. Please forgive me if I cry." "We forgive you,
Officer," I said. "And we understand why you, more than
anybody, should never touch the Prince." The goat and
I walked on. It was getting dark and we were beginning
to wonder where we would spend the night.

The Eternal Ones of the Dream

I was walking down this dirt road out
in the country. It was a sunny day in early
fall. I looked up and saw this donkey pulling
a cart coming toward me. There was no driver
nor anyone leading the donkey so far as I could
see. The donkey was just moping along. When
we met the donkey stopped and I scratched its
snout in greeting and it seemed grateful. It
seemed like a very lonely donkey, but what
donkey wouldn't feel alone on the road like that?
And then it occurred to me to see what, if anything,
was in the cart. There was only a black box,
or a coffin, about two feet long and a foot wide.
I started to lift the lid, but then I didn't,
I couldn't. I realized that this donkey was on
some woeful mission, who knows where, to the ends
of the earth, so I gave him an apple, scratched
his nose a last time and waved him on, little
man that I was.

Stray Animals

This is the beauty of being alone
toward the end of summer:
a dozen stray animals asleep on the porch
in the shade of my feet,
and the smell of leaves burning
in another neighborhood.
It is late morning,
and my forehead is alive with shadows,
some bats rock back and forth
to the rhythm of my humming,
the mimosa flutters with bees.
This is a house of unwritten poems,
this is where I am unborn.

Pastoral Scene

The wind makes a salad
of the countryside and
he who is so hungry
sits down but refuses
to eat greens. Nearby, the
river is a truck in
a hurry. He won't go
with it, however. The game
he has come to kill come
to watch him hunt himself
now. They have never felt
so safe before, so out
of place. An old predator
at last chewing on himself
is a ridiculous sight,
and the peeping white deer
are happier than they
have ever been before.

The Lost Pilot

for my father, 1922–1944

Your face did not rot
like the others—the co-pilot,
for example, I saw him

yesterday. His face is corn-
mush: his wife and daughter,
the poor ignorant people, stare

as if he will compose soon.
He was more wronged than Job.
But your face did not rot

like the others—it grew dark,
and hard like ebony;
the features progressed in their

distinction. If I could cajole
you to come back for an evening,
down from your compulsive

orbiting, I would touch you,
read your face as Dallas,
your hoodlum gunner, now,

with the blistered eyes, reads
his braille editions. I would
touch your face as a disinterested

scholar touches an original page.
However frightening, I would
discover you, and I would not

turn you in; I would not make
you face your wife, or Dallas,
or the co-pilot, Jim. You

could return to your crazy
orbiting, and I would not try
to fully understand what

it means to you. All I know
is this: when I see you,
as I have seen you at least

once every year of my life,
spin across the wilds of the sky
like a tiny, African god,

I feel dead. I feel as if I were
the residue of a stranger's life,
that I should pursue you.

My head cocked toward the sky,
I cannot get off the ground,
and, you, passing over again,

fast, perfect, and unwilling
to tell me that you are doing
well, or that it was mistake

that placed you in that world,
and me in this; or that misfortune
placed these worlds in us.

Quabbin Reservoir

All morning, skipping stones on the creamy lake,
I thought I heard a lute being played, high up,
in the birch trees, or a faun speaking French
with a Brooklyn accent. A snowy owl watched me
with half-closed eyes. "What have you done for me
philately," I wanted to ask, licking the air.
There was a village at the bottom of the lake,
and I could just make out the old post office,
and, occasionally, when the light struck it just right,
I glimpsed several mailmen swimming in or out of it,
letters and packages escaping randomly, 1938, 1937,
it didn't matter to them any longer. *Void.*
No such address. Soft blazes squirmed across the surface
and I could see their church, now home to druid squatters,
rock in the intoxicating current, as if to an ancient hymn.
And a thousand elbowing reeds conducted the drowsy band pavilion:
awake, awake, you germs of habit! Alas, I fling
my final stone, my calling card, my gift of porphyry
to the citizens of the deep, and disappear into a copse,
raving like a butterfly to a rosebud: I love you.

Dream On

Some people go their whole lives
without ever writing a single poem.
Extraordinary people who don't hesitate
to cut somebody's heart or skull open.
They go to baseball games with the greatest of ease
and play a few rounds of golf as if it were nothing.
These same people stroll into a church
as if that were a natural part of life.
Investing money is second nature to them.
They contribute to political campaigns
that have absolutely no poetry in them
and promise none for the future.
They sit around the dinner table at night
and pretend as though nothing is missing.
Their children get caught shoplifting at the mall
and no one admits that it is poetry they are missing.
The family dog howls all night,
lonely and starving for more poetry in his life.
Why is it so difficult for them to see

that, without poetry, their lives are effluvial.
Sure, they have their banquets, their celebrations,
croquet, fox hunts, their seashores and sunsets,
their cocktails on the balcony, dog races,
and all that kissing and hugging, and don't
forget the good deeds, the charity work,
nursing the baby squirrels all through the night,
filling the birdfeeders all winter,
helping the stranger change her tire.
Still, there's that disagreeable exhalation
from decaying matter, subtle but ever present.
They walk around erect like champions.
They are smooth-spoken, urbane and witty.
When alone, rare occasion, they stare
into the mirror for hours, bewildered.
There was something they meant to say, but didn't:
"And if we put the statue of the rhinoceros
next to the tweezers, and walk around the room three times,
learn to yodel, shave our heads, call
our ancestors back from the dead—"
poetry-wise it's still a bust, bankrupt.
You haven't scribbled a syllable of it.
You're a nowhere man misfiring
the very essence of your life, flustering
nothing from nothing and back again.
The hereafter may not last all that long.
Radiant childhood sweetheart,
secret code of everlasting joy and sorrow,

fanciful pen strokes beneath the eyelids:
all day, all night meditation, knot of hope,
kernel of desire, pure ordinariness of life,
seeking, through poetry, a benediction
or a bed to lie down on, to connect, reveal,
explore, to imbue meaning on the day's extravagant labor.
And yet it's cruel to expect too much.
It's a rare species of bird
that refuses to be categorized,
Its song is barely audible.
It is like a dragonfly in a dream—
here, then there, then here again,
low-flying amber-wing darting upward
and then out of sight.
And the dream has a pain in its heart
the wonders of which are manifold, or so the story is told.

I Sat at My Desk and Contemplated All That I Had Accomplished

I sat at my desk and contemplated all that I had accomplished this year. I had won the hot dog eating contest on Rhode Island. No, I hadn't. I was just kidding. I was the arm wrestling champion in Portland, Maine. False. I caught the largest boa constrictor in Southern Brazil. In my dreams. I built the largest house out of matchsticks in all the United States. Wow! I caught a wolf by its tail. Yummy. I married the Princess of Monaco. Can you believe it? I fell off of Mount Everest. Ouch! I walked back up again. It was tiring. Snore. I set a record for sitting in my chair and snoring louder than anybody. Awake! I set a record for swimming from one end of my bath to the other in No Count, Nebraska. Blurb. I read a book written by a dove. Great! I slept in my chair all day and all night for thirty days. Whew! I ate a cheeseburger every day for a year. I never want to do that again. A trout bit me when I was washing the dishes. But I couldn't catch him. I flew over my hometown and didn't recognize anyone. That's how long it's been. A policeman stopped me on the street and said he was sorry. He was looking for someone who looked just like me. What are the chances?

Rescue

For the first time the only
thing you are likely to break

is everything because
it is a dangerous

venture. Danger invites
rescue—I call it loving.

We've got a good thing
going—I call it rescue.

Nicest thing ever to come
between steel cobwebs, we hope

so. A few others should get
around to it, I can't understand

it. There is plenty of room,
clean windows, we start our best

engines, a-rumm . . . everything is
relevant. I call it loving.